39 ESL Review Games and Activities:

For Teenagers and Adults

Jackie Bolen

+

Jennifer Booker Smith

Table of Contents

About the Author: Jackie Bolen..4
About the Author: Jennifer Booker Smith..5
About the Editor: Jack Alss..6
Speaking + Listening Review Games and Activities....................................7
    Ball Toss..7
    Board Games...9
    Dictogloss..11
    Infographic Presentation...12
    Passive Dice Game...15
    Password...16
    QR Code Hunt..19
    Quiz Circles..20
    Quiz Show Review Game..22
    Rock-Scissor-Paper..24
    Role-plays...25
    Running Dictation..28
    Steal the Eraser...30
    Survey Activities..31
    Tic-Tac-Toe..34
    Typhoon..35
    Vocabulary Checkers..37
    Vocabulary Pictionary..38
    Vocabulary Poker Face...40
Reading Review Games and Activities...42
    Concentration...42
    Correction Relay..43
    Disappearing Words...44
    Irregular Go Fish..45
    Odd One Out..46
    Story Timeline..47
    What's the Main Idea?...48
    Where Are They Now?..49
    Word-Definition Match 50
Writing Review Games and Activities..52
    Adjective or Adverb Modifier Posters...52
    Chapter Response...53
    Got to Hand it to You...54
    Haiku Activity..55
    Is that Sentence Correct?...56
    Make a Sentence..57
    Proofreading/Editing..58
    Review Race...58
    Textbook Part of Speech Race...59
    Vocabulary Roll and Write...60

Worksheet Relay...62
Before You Go...64

Copyright 2015 by Jackie Bolen + Jennifer Booker Smith

All rights reserved. No part of this publication may be reproduced, distributed, or transmitted in any form or by any means, including photocopying, recording or other electronic or mechanical means without the prior written permission of the publisher, except in the case of brief quotations in critical reviews and certain other non-commercial uses permitted by copyright law. For permission requests, write to the publisher/author at the address below.

Jackie Bolen: wealthyenglishteacher@gmail.com.

About the Author: Jackie Bolen

I've been teaching English in South Korea for a decade to every level and type of student and I've taught every age from kindergarten kids to adults. Most of my time has centered around teaching at two universities: five years at a science and engineering school out in the rice paddies of Chungcheongnam-Do, and four years at a major university in Busan where I now teach high level classes for students majoring in English. In my spare time, you can usually find me outside surfing, biking, hiking or on the hunt for the most delicious kimchi I can find.

In case you were wondering what my academic qualifications are, I hold a Master of Arts in Psychology. During my time in Korea I've successfully completed both the Cambridge CELTA and DELTA certification programs. With the combination of almost ten years teaching ESL/EFL learners of all ages and levels, and the more formal teaching qualifications I've obtained, I have a solid foundation on which to offer teaching advice. I truly hope that you find this book useful and would love it if you sent me an email with any questions or feedback that you might have—I'll always take the time to personally respond (wealthyenglishteacher@gmail.com).

Jackie Bolen around the Internet

ESL Speaking (www.eslspeaking.org)

Jackie Bolen (www.jackiebolen.com)

Twitter: @bolen_jackie

Email: wealthyenglishteacher@gmail.com

About the Author: Jennifer Booker Smith

I have a Master of Education in TESOL and have spent fifteen years teaching students of all ages in Korea, from two-year-old preschoolers barely out of diapers to businessmen and even a semester as a teacher trainer at an education university. However, my greatest love is the middle primary grades—I left a fairly cushy teacher trainer position to return to the elementary classroom. In that age group, I've taught all ability levels from false beginner to near-native returnees.

During my time in the classroom, I've created countless board and card games and other resources. In this book, you'll find some of the vocabulary activities that I have used successfully (I've tried plenty which weren't successful!) in a variety of settings; these are the ones I've used again and again because they actually work.

When I'm not teaching, like Jackie, you can often find me hiking. I've taken up running recently and will soon be running my third half marathon. Teaching takes up a lot more "free" time than non-teachers will ever realize, so it's important to recharge the batteries and being outside is my favorite way to do just that.

You can get in touch with me by emailing jenniferteacher@gmail.com. I'd love to hear from you and help you with your classes in any way that I can.

About the Editor: Jack Alss

Jack Alss is the nom de guerre for a fellow educator/editor in the trenches. He started teaching at the age of 16, got a scholarship (at a university as far away from home as possible!); wrote an essay that landed him a job at a national magazine as journalist/editor; and managed to find time to also dabble in home renovation, garden design, blacksmithing; and writing and editing leaflets, reports, and service and course manuals for the military, churches, banks, and interior designers to name a few. Teaching in Asia the past 14 years, Jack has extensive knowledge of the EFL, EAL, and ESL scene, and his students range typically from high school students to top level management at internationally recognized companies. You are welcome to contact him at jackalss49@gmail.com

Speaking + Listening Review Games and Activities

Ball Toss

Skills: Reading/Writing/Speaking/Listening

Time: 5-10 minutes

Level: Beginner to Intermediate

Materials: Lightweight ball (such as a beach ball) with questions written on it

This game has many variations. One variation I have used with great success is writing questions on a beach ball. I use a whiteboard marker to write on the ball, but let it dry thoroughly before class, so it doesn't smudge but it can be washed clean and reused with different questions later. Students gently toss the ball to one another and read aloud and answer the question under their right thumb. A more complex variation is: Student A reads/asks the question, tosses the ball to Student B, who answers that question, then asks the question under their right thumb, and tosses the ball to Student C, who answers Student B's question.

Ball toss is quite a versatile activity and can be used with just about anything that you want to review.

If you don't have a ball handy, you can crumple up a piece of paper to use as a ball. Ask a question and toss the ball to a student. That student must answer and ask a question (the same question for true beginners or related question, if higher level), then toss the "ball" to the next student. If you want the students to ask different questions, you should give them a topic (daily routine, hobbies, etc.) or grammar pattern to use.

If you want to make sure all students have equal turns, have students sit down after catching the ball. If you have more than 10-12 students in your class, you may want to divide them into groups, each with their own ball, so students aren't waiting long periods between turns. This will also increase student talking time.

Teaching Tips:

At the end, you may want to ask students questions about other students' answers. Let students know before they begin that they need to listen closely to each other's answers. This will make them more likely to pay attention between their own turns and, of course, provide additional listening and speaking practice.

Generally, this activity can be used with any class size: you can use it for larger classes, as long as their level is move advanced, simply because they will be better suited to working in small groups with less attention needed from you. If you have a class of 30 beginners, you might want to simply toss the ball and ask a question, rather than require them to read it, and have each student repeat the same question as they toss the ball. After 10-12 students have asked and answered the same question, take the ball and toss it to a different student, asking a new question.

Procedure:

1. Prepare a beach ball by writing questions on it. Allow enough time for the ink to dry before class. No beach ball version: crumple up a piece of scrap paper with the questions written on it.

2. Have students stand in a circle (as much as possible). If your class is large, divide students into groups of 10-12.

Variation A:

When a student catches the ball, they must read out the question under their right thumb. They answer their own question and toss the ball to another student.

Variation B:

When Student A catches the ball, they ask the question under their right thumb to Student B. When Student B answers, A tosses them the ball. Student B asks Student C the question under their right thumb and so on.

No Prep Variation:

The teacher asks a question and tosses the ball to Student A. Student A answers, asks Student B a question, and tosses them the ball.

Board Games

Skills: Reading/Speaking
Time: 25-40 minutes
Level: Beginner to Advanced
Materials: Board game sheet and token for each student (a coin or eraser)

Board Games often come in the "teacher's resource book" that goes along with your textbook and if this is the case, you're in luck because no prep will be required but you'll have a solid activity that your students will probably love and it has the added bonus of being extremely student-centered. However, don't worry if there isn't a pre-made game in the textbook because it's easier than you might think to make your own. It will only take 5-10 minutes once you get a bit of experience doing it.

Use questions based on the grammar and/or vocabulary that you've been studying during the previous classes. Have some fun squares, such as, "Switch positions with the person on your right" or, "Go back 5 spaces." The style I typically use is a question of some kind where the student has to speak one or two sentences in response to it. The other students in the group listen for incorrect answers, in which case the student has to move back the number that they "rolled." You can use dice (which gets loud), two coins (2 heads = 5, 1 head + 1 tail = 3, 2 tails = 1), or a number sheet where students close their eyes and move their pen to choose a number.

Teaching Tips:

Board games have their own lexical set and it may be the first time many of your students have ever played a board game in English so it's useful to do some pre-teaching. Before you play, you can teach them some key phrases and encourage them to speak only English (it's your turn, go ahead, your roll, pass the dice, let's ask the teacher, etc.).

Dice are my least favorite way to "roll" because they fall off the desk, roll around the room and they can also be very loud. Using coins or a paper sheet with a pen is much more controlled.

If students disagree about whether an answer is correct or incorrect, you can make a joke and tell them not to fight but just to ask you to be the referee. You should think carefully about your game though and make most of the questions easy enough so that there are obvious correct answers. If not, your class time will be very stressful if you have a big class and many groups demanding your attention at the same time.

Before I give the winner of each group a little prize, I'll often make them answer one or two final questions, which I usually take from the game board. It's a good way to review correct vocabulary and/or grammar use with the class in case any group has been off-base but you didn't catch it. A key component of learning language is hearing it and using it again, and again, and again. Help your students do this in class by doing quick reviews together at the end of activities.

Procedure:

1. Hand out the "game boards" as well as dice or coins to groups of 3-5 students. Have each student provide their own token—it can be an eraser, a key or a small piece of paper.

2. The students can do rock-scissor-paper to see who goes first. The first student uses the dice or coins to find the number of spaces they will move ahead. That student answers the question and if correct, they stay on that space but if incorrect, they move back the number of spaces that they rolled.

3. The next student rolls the dice and answers a question and so on.

4. The game continues until one student reaches the final square on the game, or until the time is up. If the group doesn't finish, the winner is the students who has made it the furthest.

Dictogloss

Skills: Speaking/Listening

Time: 10-15 minutes

Level: Intermediate to Advanced

Materials: A short story

This is a simple activity for higher level students that helps them practice their listening and memory skills, as well as substituting vocabulary words if the original word is no longer accessible to them. To use this as a review activity, make up a short story with key vocabulary or grammar that you've been studying. Or, you can often find something suitable in the textbook.

Tell the story 1-3 times, depending on the student level and of course you can also vary your speaking speed to make this activity easier or harder. Once you are done telling the story, students will have to go in groups of 2-3 to retell the story. Emphasize that they won't be able to recreate the exact story that you told, but that they should try their best to keep the meaning the same. Each team can pair up with another team to compare. Then, tell the original story again so students can see how they did.

This activity works well as a writing activity too.

Teaching Tips:

It's very helpful for students to compare answers with a partner before they have to say anything in front of the class so be sure to put them in partners or groups of three to work together on this activity. It's useful for the weaker students to have a stronger student getting them up to speed. It also gives students confidence that they're on the right track and they're less nervous to share their answers with the class.

If you use something "scandalous," it will make the activity a lot more fun! Of course, it should still be appropriate so just picture your boss observing your class to decide if you should use it or not.

Procedure:

1. Prepare a short story which you'll read to your students.

2. Put students in groups of two or three and read the story to them.

3. Students try to remember the details of the story and compare with their group. I usually only allow them to do this by speaking.

4. Read the story again and students attempt to recreate the story more closely, again by speaking.

5. Read the story again (depending on level and difficulty of story) and students again attempt to recreate it, even more closely.

6. Elicit a couple of teams to tell their story to the class (in a small class). Or, put two teams together and they tell their stories to each other (in a larger class). The teacher can move among the groups and monitor them.

7. Read the story one final time for students to compare their own versions.

Infographic Presentation

Skills: Reading/Writing/Speaking/Listening

Time: 1+ hour

Level: High-Beginner to Advanced

Materials: Internet access, PowerPoint

Optional Materials: Video camera

Presentations are a regular feature of ESL classes, but your student may get overwhelmed at the thought of first creating and then presenting a full-length speech. Infographics have become a common way of presenting information, and your student can create and use one to provide the "meat" of an informative oral presentation. This will also provide an opportunity to research a topic in English. If your student works in an office, he or she is likely to use PowerPoint at work, so the combination of something familiar (PPT) with something new (English presentation) should reduce stress.

Have your student choose a topic of interest to them that has several data points. For example, if he/she has a favorite team, he/she can find the team's current ranking, average points per game, number of championships, and so on to populate the infographic. The student should begin the project by researching several data points and finding an image or two online to use for decoration. If you want to use this specifically as a review activity, you can require that students choose from a narrow range of topics that you've studied in class. Or, you can require that students use certain grammar points or vocabulary during the course of their presentation.

To create the infographic, the student will need to reset the margins to create the long, narrow look of an infographic. This is done by choosing a blank layout and changing the slide from landscape to portrait then adjusting the margins. Start with 10"/25cm by 30"/75cm and adjust if necessary. Your student can use images, Smart Art, and/or charts to present the data he/she will report. However, you may want to give your student a time limit for choosing a layout or have him/her make a sketch before opening PowerPoint, because the number of options can become a time waster.

Once the layout has been chosen, your student will need to fill in the data. If he/she is using charts, Excel will automatically to fill them in. Don't worry, it's pretty self-explanatory and the end result is right there for the student to see while working. Once the images are all in place, the student should add a brief explanation of each image. All images and text boxes can be resized, and the entire slide can be resized by adjusting the margins, if there is more (or less) information than expected.

When the student is satisfied with the infographic, it can be saved as a JPEG. This will probably have taken an entire lesson, so the presentation will be in the next lesson. You should tailor the focus of the presentation to your student's level and needs. A lower-level student may just need to practice speaking without a script. Higher-level students may need to practice the use of gestures or inflection.

For the presentation of the infographic, pull up the saved image and have the student sit or stand next to the computer to present the data to you. A lower-level student may do best seated next to you with both of you looking at the screen. Being able to look at the image (and not having you looking directly at your student) should reduce quite a bit of stress. After doing several presentation activities, the student's confidence will hopefully increase and he/she won't need such modifications.

Teaching Tips:

If your student does not use PowerPoint at work and is not familiar with it (or if you do not want to spend an entire lesson making an infographic), you may want to have the student find an existing infographic online to present.

A video of the presentation can be helpful for your student. When students see and hear themselves, they can more easily see the areas that need improvement.

Procedure:

1. Have your student choose a topic of interest that would have several data points to

research and present.

2. Have the student make a sketch of the planned infographic.

3. Using PowerPoint, have the student make the infographic (use a blank layout, in portrait, with the margins set to 10"/25cm by 30"/75cm).

4. In the next lesson, have the student present the infographic to you. According to the student's level, have him/her focus on speaking without a script, using gestures, or inflection, etc.

5. Review the presentation.

Passive Dice Game

Skills: Speaking/Listening

Time: 10 minutes

Level: High Beginner to Intermediate

Materials: For each pair/ group of students: 1 vocabulary die and 1 time die made from two milk cartons each

This activity requires quite a bit of preparation, but you can make it a pre-game activity if you wish and get the students to help you make it. Before playing, you will need to make the pairs of dice:

- four milk cartons, washed and completely dry

- clear tape

- six time words/ phrases and six vocabulary words printed and cut to fit the side of the carton

1. Cut the tops off of the milk cartons and join two together by indenting the sides of one at the opening and pushing the open end into the open end of another. Repeat to create all pairs of dice.

2. Secure the two cartons together with tape.

3. On die one, attach one vocab word per side. On die two, attach one time word (for example, yesterday or last year) on each side. Tape securely.

In class, divide students into groups of 2-4. Each student will take turns rolling the dice and making a passive sentence using both of the words or phrases showing face up.

Students should continue to take turns until time is up. If you wish to include a writing element, you can have students write the sentences they make.

Teaching Tips:

If you do not have access to a large number of single serving milk cartons, you can easily find printable dice templates online. Print, enlarge to the size you need, fill in the squares, assemble, and cover with wide, clear tape until sturdy enough to withstand repeated use. You can use clear contact paper or self-laminating paper, but I find it to be quite difficult with an empty paper cube.

Procedure:

1. In advance, make the milk carton dice according to the directions above.

2. Divide students into groups of 2-4.

3. Have each student take turns rolling the dice and making a passive sentence using both of the words or phrases showing face up until time is up.

4. If you wish to include a writing element, you can have students write the sentences they make.

Password

Skills: Speaking/Listening

Time: 10-20 minutes

Level: Beginner to Intermediate

Materials: List of words, whiteboard

This activity helps students review vocabulary and practice an important skill: describing something they don't know the word for. Divide students into two groups. The groups will alternate sending a team member to stand at the front of the class with his/her back to the board. Write a word over the person's head, so the team mates can see it but the student cannot. The team must give that person hints until he/she guesses the word or time runs out (20-30 seconds). The team with the most points wins.

Variation:

Have one team's turn last until they run out of time (2-4 minutes) and then switch. This gives an advantage for correctly guessing more quickly. Pause the clock between answers so a new team member can take the hot seat.

Procedure:

1. In advance, prepare a list of words. These can be vocabulary taught in class or just words you expect your students to know.
2. Divide class into two groups.
3. Have groups alternate sending a member to the front of the class, or give each group a time limit of 2-4 minutes and rotate team members as soon as one guesses a word, until time is up.
4. Write a word on the whiteboard over that person's head, so his/her team can see it, but the student cannot.
5. That student's team must give the person hints until he/she guesses the word or time runs out (20-30 seconds).
6. The team with the most points at the end of all the rounds is the winner.

Poster Project Group Presentation

Skills: Speaking/Listening

Time: 5-10 hours preparation, 1 hour presentation time (depending on class size)

Level: Beginner to Advanced

Materials: Large poster paper

If you want to do some task-based learning in your class, this is an excellent one to do. Put your students in groups of 2-4 and assign a topic or theme. If you're studying about food, you could tell your students to choose a popular food in their country. If your class is about current events or social issues, each group could choose one of those. You can have students do a presentation on just about any topic that you've been studying in class. You may want to require that students use key grammatical features or words from a vocabulary list a certain number of times.

Then, students will have to make a poster with some pictures and a minimal amount of text. Emphasize the minimal text because if you don't, many of the posters will be filled with a large amount of text that is impossible to read. It's a good idea to draw a model poster on the whiteboard and draw big pictures with examples of writing size and content. You can point these things out as you give instructions.

Once the poster is complete (give class time, or for homework), the group will make a presentation about the topic. I emphasize that each group member must talk for an equal amount of time and that they must memorize their presentation and cannot read from a paper. Finally, I ask them to prepare a few quiz questions (3-5) for their classmates to test and see if they were listening! You can also include some Q & A time if your class is outgoing and they won't be too shy to do this.

Teaching Tips:

This is an excellent activity to use if you want to focus on stress and intonation with your students. You can show them how to use these things to emphasize the key points, signal a transition or signal what is old and what is new information.

You could also consider introducing some markers that are present in more formal kinds of spoken discourse such as this one. For example, there are standard ways to introduce a topic (Today, I'm going to talk about _____), develop an idea (I'll talk about three main points related to this), transition into another idea (Now that you've heard about A, I'd like to talk about B), or conclude a presentation (Remember the most important points are _____.)

While not a lot of preparation is required for this since your students are doing most of the work, you need to be really clear in your head about what your expectations are and you also need to convey this really clearly to your students. If you don't, you're likely to be disappointed in the results, but it will be your fault and not the students'. It can be helpful to prepare a list of "Top 10 Dos and Don'ts" on a handout or on a class website or *Facebook* group.

It is extremely important to get students to memorize their speeches and to ensure this, you can allocate a large amount of points (20-30%) to it if the assignment is graded. If you don't, the presentation will likely be terrible and will often consist of simply reading from a PowerPoint or a piece of paper. I do however tell my students to bring their script up to the front with them and they can look one time per person without any penalty in case they truly forget what they need to say.

Procedure:

1. Put students into groups and assign a topic.

2. Give explicit instructions about what is required of them regarding the poster and the presentation.

3. Have students prepare the poster and the presentation, either in class or for homework.

4. Students do their presentation in front of the class.

5. The students ask their classmates some quiz questions based on what they talked about.

6. Question and answer time (optional).

QR Code Hunt

Skills: Speaking/Listening

Time: 15-60 minutes

Level: Beginner to Intermediate

Materials: Internet access, printer, tape/Blu-tack, student phones with QR code reader apps installed

This activity requires a bit more prep than others, but (as of writing) the novelty factor is high! Classtools.net makes it easy to put together a QR code hunt, so don't worry if you haven't used QR codes before—if you can type, you can do this activity. This activity will require some creativity in order to put together some challenging review questions.

Procedure:

1. In advance, write your questions in a Word document. These can be discussion questions, trivia questions (pub quiz), or you can pre-test student levels, particularly if you are teaching a subject class.

2. Go to http://www.classtools.net/QR/ and copy and paste.

3. Create the QR codes and print.

4. Post the printouts in various places around the class, or better yet, a larger area.

5. Before dividing students into groups, make sure at least one member of each group has a QR code reader on their phone. If not, give them a minute to download an app—there are plenty of them and most adult students will already have one.

6. Divide students into groups of 3-4 and give them a time limit to find and answer all of the questions.

7. Particularly if you plan to assess student levels, as an option you can have students write the questions they find, and their answers.

8. Wrap up the class with a group discussion of the answers.

Quiz Circles

Skills: Speaking/Listening

Time: 5-15 minutes

Level: Beginner to Intermediate

Materials: Timer or buzzer, index cards with questions and answers

Optional Materials: Noise control app

This is a spoken review exercise which gets students up and moving in a controlled way. It's a good alternative to mingling if your students tend to choose the same friends every time you have a mingling activity. This activity can be done sitting if you have movable chairs and the space to put them in circles, but standing is easier. In advance, you will need to prepare one index card per student with a quiz question and answer written on the same side, so their partner can't read it. Alternatively, you can begin class by giving each student a blank index card and having them create one question and answer.

Create the circles by dividing students into two groups. One group will be the outside circle, which will be stationary. The other will be the inside group, which will rotate. If you have an odd number of students, you can either join in or have the left over student join the outside circle and work with a partner. Have the outside circle face inward and space themselves out as much as possible, then have the inside circle stand in the middle facing a student in the outside circle. Let the students know that each time the buzzer rings, the inside group should shift one student to their right.

When you start the timer, each student in the outside circle should ask their partner in the inside circle their question. The inside circle should answer, then ask their own question. If either answers incorrectly, their partner should tell them the correct answer. They should continue moving around until each person has answered each question.

Teaching Tips:

Set the timer according to the level of the students and the difficulty of the specific task. If they are giving definitions to vocabulary words, they will need less time than if they are answering a question about a story you have read in class. Lower level students will also need more thinking time. In any case, keep the maximum time to about a minute to keep things moving.

You may want to let students know when time is half through, so they can switch, or you can have the outside circle ask their questions on the first pass and the inside circles ask theirs on the second pass.

If your class is quite large or the pool of questions low, have two sets of circles. Keeping in mind that literally half of the class will speaking at any given time, you may want to use a classroom noise control app, especially if there are nearby classes which may be disturbed. The older the students, the more awareness they will have of "inside voices", so some gentle reminders may be all that is necessary to keep things to a dull roar.

Procedure:

1. In advance, prepare one index card per student with a quiz question and answer written on the same side, so their partner can't read it.
2. In class, create the circles by dividing students into two groups.
3. Have the outside circle face inward and space themselves out as much as possible, then have the inside circle stand in the middle facing a student in the outside circle.
4. If you have an odd number of students, you can either join in or have the left over student join the outside circle and work with a partner.
5. Let the students know that each time the buzzer rings, the inside group should shift one student to their right.
6. When you start the timer, each student in the outside circle should ask their partner in the inside circle their question. The inside circle should answer, then ask their own question.
7. If either answers incorrectly, their partner should tell them the correct answer.
8. They should continue moving around until each person has answered each question.

Quiz Show Review Game

Skills: Speaking/Listening

Time: 30-45 minutes

Level: Beginner to Intermediate

Materials: PowerPoint chart, or whiteboard and questions

This is a "Jeopardy" style quiz game, which is useful for teenagers all the way up to adults. It works especially well as a review game before a test. Although most teachers spend a lot of time making this game by using PowerPoint, it really isn't necessary and you can simply write up the grid on the whiteboard before class starts in less than a minute. It should only take you 5-10 minutes to prepare the questions if you're very familiar with the material so it really is a low-prep game.

Make up categories based on whatever you have been studying. For example: "vocab, can/can't, movies, body, etc." Think of questions that range from easy ($100) to difficult ($500). Put the students in groups of 3-4 and they have to pick their category and question. The students can pick whatever they want, but the key is that if they get it correct, they get the points. If wrong, they get minus that number. I put in a few +/- $500/$1000 and choose your own wager (up to $1000) to make it more interesting and give the lower level teams a chance to catch up.

There are a few different ways that you can get students to answer questions such as being the first entire team to put their hands up, or hit a buzzer but that can get pretty chaotic. Instead, I do this activity in a more controlled fashion with each team choosing questions in order, one at a time.

One very fun category that I like to include is "random," where I ask any sort of question that we didn't specifically talk about in class. It's more like a general knowledge or trivia category.

You could also include a category called, "All about _____" where you ask the students questions about yourself. Only include those things that you've mentioned in class before and observant students will be able to answer.

Teachings Tips:

Something I do to make it more interesting for the other teams who are not answering the question is tell the students that some of the questions from the game are actual questions on the exam that they're usually doing the next week. I don't think I've ever had so many students paying such close attention to anything before! And of course, put in a few of the game questions on the test to reward those who were listening closely.

If you want to make this game more student-centered and also practice writing and questions forms, you can get the students to make the questions. Put the students into groups of 3-4 and give them the general categories. Then, for each category, they have to submit one easy, one medium and one difficult question. Compile their questions and play the game in the next class you have together. A team might be lucky and get their own question, but it shouldn't happen too often.

Procedure:

1. Make a list of review questions. This depends on the number of categories but 25 works well (5x5).
2. Make sure each team gets asked an equal number of questions.
3. Put students into teams of 3-6 and do rock-scissor-paper to see who goes first.
4. The first team chooses a category and a price. Ask them that question. If correct, they get the points and you can eliminate that question from your board. If incorrect, they lose those points and that question remains in play so that another team can answer it.
5. The next team chooses a question. Follow the same procedure as above.
6. Continue the game until most or all of the questions are gone and all the teams have had a chance to answer an equal number of questions.

Rock-Scissor-Paper

Skills: Reading/Writing/Speaking/Listening

Time: 20 minutes

Level: Beginner to Intermediate

Materials: Question and answer papers (5 per student)

This is an excellent review activity to do before a test for lower level classes where there are well-defined, closed type questions and answers. On separate papers, make matching questions and answers. Give each student five random papers with a mix of both questions and answers. They have to walk around the class to find their "match." Once they do, they can rock-scissor-paper and the winner takes both papers and those papers are "out." In order to increase student talking time, my rule is that students cannot read each other's papers but must find the matching papers only through speaking. If I see students reading, I enforce a penalty of some kind, where I usually take away one of their matches. The students with the most points (matches) after a certain period of time are the winners.

Teaching Tip:

Try to design questions that have unambiguous questions and answers. I mean that each question should have one very specific answer and not be possible for other papers. Make sure you do a demonstration with a couple examples before you start so your students understand the game. I'll usually set aside a couple of matches for my demo and arrange it so that two good students get one part, while I keep the corresponding one. Then I "find" the matches.

Procedure:

1. Prepare matching question and answer papers using unambiguous questions and answers. Cut them out into single strips of paper (questions and answers are separate).

2. Give each student five random papers, in a mix of questions and answers.

3. Students walk around the class, finding their "match." They can do this only by speaking and not by reading each other's papers.

4. Once they find a match, they do rock-scissor-paper.

5. The winner keeps both papers and that set is finished.

6. The winner is the student with the most sets after the allotted time. If there are more than two or three students who are the "winners," you can reduce this by having a final rock-scissor-paper showdown.

7. Check carefully at the end of the game to ensure that papers are indeed matches. It can be a good teachable moment to explain why a potential match is incorrect if a mistake is made.

Role-plays

Skills: Writing/Reading/Speaking/Listening

Time Required: 20-40 minutes

Level: Beginner to Intermediate

Materials: None

Partner role-plays are an excellent way to get students practicing using new vocabulary in a real-life context. They make a great review activity for the end of a class, or at the beginning of the next one. Give the students a conversation starter to get them going. For example, if you're talking about *feelings* in class that day, you can use:

A: Hey _____, how are you doing?

B: I'm great, how are you?

A: I'm _____ (sad, embarrassed, angry, bored, etc.). ***Anything besides, "I'm fine, thank you, and you?" is good. ***

B: Oh? What's wrong?

A: _____.

B: _____.

Another context that I often use this activity with is *illness or injury*. For example:

A: Hey _____, you don't look (sound) so good! What's wrong?

B: Oh yeah, I'm not good. I _____.

A: Really? _____.

B: _____.

A: _____.

One final context that I use this with is *excuses*. For example:

A: Hey _____, you're _____ minutes late!

B: I'm really sorry. I've been/I had to _____.

A: Hmmm . . . _____.

Give the students about ten minutes to write the conversation with their partner. You can adjust the number of lines and how detailed of a starter you give to suit the ability level of your students. For lower-level students, it can be helpful to have a word bank relevant to the context on the whiteboard so that the writing portion of this activity doesn't get too long (you can also provide them with a detailed, fill-in-the-blank script). Then, the students memorize their conversation (no papers when speaking!), and do a role-play in front of their classmates if you have a small class of fewer than ten. Remember that you should try to maximize the amount of time students are talking. If you have a larger class, there are a few different ways to handle this. You could get pairs to come up to your desk and show you their conversation while the other students are working on something else, you could use it as a speaking test of some kind, each pair could join with one or two other groups and perform for them, or finally you could have students make a video of themselves and send you the link or upload it to *YouTube*.

I really like this activity because it's perfect for lower-level students who want to practice "conversation" but don't quite have the skills to do this on their own, and it's also a good way to force your advanced students to use some new grammar or vocabulary that you're teaching.

Teaching Tips:

Having your students make conversations is very useful for practicing functional language and speaking sub-skills. I usually choose one or two functions to mention when I'm giving the instructions for the activity and provide a bit of coaching and language input surrounding that, depending on the level—beginners will need more help.

The functions that fit particularly well with partner conversations include agreeing, disagreeing, apologizing, and asking advice. The sub-skills that you can emphasize are things like turn-taking, initiating a conversation, speaking for an appropriate length of time, stress and intonation, responding (really?), and cohesive devices, particularly noun pronoun reference: A: I saw a movie last night. B: Which one did you see? A. I saw Iron Man. It was good.

This is one of the most useful things you can do in your conversation classes, especially for beginner or intermediate students so make sure you try it out at least once or twice over the course of a semester. It gives your students a chance to have a real conversation which will build a lot of confidence but they won't have the pressure of coming up with something to say on the spot. That said, it gets boring if you do this every class; I generally do it about once a month for a class that meets twice a week over the course of a semester.

Procedure:

1. Prepare a conversation starter based on what you are teaching.
2. (Optional) Pre-teach some language that students could use, if you haven't done that already in your lesson.
3. Write the conversation starter on the whiteboard, PowerPoint, or on a handout.
4. Have students complete the conversation in pairs. Then, they must prepare to speak by memorizing and adding in stress and intonation. You could give some individual help to each pair to assist them in knowing what to stress and how to do it.
5. Have students stand up and "perform" their conversation if you have a small class. In larger classes, there are a few other options (see above).
6. Reward teams for interesting conversations, good acting (no reading), and correct use of grammar/vocabulary that you were teaching that day.

Running Dictation

Skills: Writing/Listening/Speaking/Reading

Time: 15 minutes

Level: Beginner to Advanced

Materials: The "dictation" + some way to attach it to the walls or board.

This is one of my favorite activities which covers reading, writing, listening and speaking. There are a wide variety of English styles you can choose: poems, song lyrics, a short story, famous quotes—the list is almost limitless. For example, you might make up a story or conversation a few sentences long (no more than ten). I will often use this as a warm-up at the beginning of a class to review material from previous classes. I'll include grammar and vocabulary in the story or conversation that I've recently taught. Whatever you do, put each sentence on a strip of paper, and you can also put another strip of paper on top to prevent cheating. Put these around the classroom in various locations.

The students will be in teams of two. One person is the reader and one is the writer. The reader gets up and reads a bit of the passage and comes and tells it to the writer. They go back to remember more of it and so on and so on. At the end, the students have to put the song or conversation in order. If you have beginner students, make sure it's obvious enough what the correct order should be. Intermediate and advanced students can handle something with a bit of ambiguity. When they're done, I'll check their writing and if there aren't many mistakes plus the order is correct, that team is the winner. How many mistakes you allow depends on the level of your students.

Tell your students before the activity starts that standing at the strip of paper and then yelling to their partner instead of walking over to them is not allowed or they will be disqualified.

Teaching Tips:

Make sure you let your students know what cheating is (yelling, the "reader/speaker" touching the pen, using their phone camera) and if that happens their team will automatically be disqualified.

Make sure you move beyond simply dictating the sentences down onto the paper into dealing with meaning as well. You can do this by requiring students to put the conversation, song or poem in the correct order. They can write "1, 2, 3, 4" beside each sentence instead of re-writing them. Make sure whatever you choose has some sort of logical order to it. Alternatively, if you choose something that doesn't really have an order, you could skip this step.

Procedure:

1. Prepare a simple story or conversation and put each sentence on a strip of paper.
2. Put the papers around the classroom on the wall, equally spaced out.
3. Divide the students into pairs: one writer and one reader.
4. The reader stands up, walks to the station and reads a paper, then goes back to the writer and tells what they read to the writer, who must write it. The reader can go back to a single paper as many times as required.
5. This procedure of reading, speaking, listening, and writing continues until the team has all the sentences down on their paper.
6. The two students put the story or conversation in the correct order.
7. The teacher can check for accuracy and meaning and decide if it's acceptable, or not.

Steal the Eraser

Skills: Listening/Speaking

Time: 10-15 minutes

Level: Beginner to Intermediate

Materials: 2 chairs, a table or desk, eraser

Divide the students into two teams. Have two desks at the front of the class, facing each other with an eraser in the middle of the two desks. One student from each team comes and sits in the hot seat. Rotate through the class so that all the students get a chance to play at least once. You then ask a question of some sort, which you should prepare beforehand (one round = one question/2 students. Two rounds = one question/student. Include a few extras for a "bonus" round). The first person that grabs the eraser can try to answer the question. A helpful rule is that the student can take the eraser whenever they want, but the teacher stops talking as soon as the eraser is touched. The student then has ten seconds to answer as you count down on your fingers. If correct, they get one point. If not, the other player gets a chance to answer the question after you repeat the full question one more time.

To make it even more exciting or if one team is behind by a lot of points, have a "Bonus Round," where the teams pick their best three players and each question is worth three points.

Teaching Tips:

Emphasize that the first student to touch the eraser must take it in order to prevent any chaos. I also require students to keep their fingers on the edge of their desks when I begin the question. It's really important to stop talking the instant one student touches the eraser. If not, students will just grab the eraser and wait for you to finish the question, which is really unfair. It's best to use questions that have very well-defined answers so you don't have to make any judgement calls because half the class will be unhappy with you no matter what decision you make.

Procedure:

1. Prepare two desks facing each at the front of the class, with an eraser in the middle.
2. Divide students into two teams.
3. Each team sends up one person to the front and they sit at the desks. I don't let students choose the person for each round but simply make them go in the order that they are sitting.
4. The teacher asks a question (prepare the list beforehand), but stops speaking once the eraser is touched. Alternatively, you can have each team appoint a captain who takes turns reading the prepared list of questions in order to increase student talking time.
5. The first player to touch the eraser must answer the question within ten seconds. Count

down the time on your fingers.

6. If correct, he/she gets one point and the next two people come up to the front for another question.

7. If incorrect, the teacher reads the question (in full) one more time and the opposing player gets a chance to answer the question within ten seconds.

8. If correct, they get one point. If incorrect, both players sit down and the next pair comes up. You can share the correct answer with the class before saying a new question.

9. Continue until all students have had a chance to play at least once.

Survey Activities

Skills: Speaking/Listening/Writing/Reading

Time: 15-30 minutes

Level: High-Beginner to Advanced

Materials: Survey handout

Survey activities are a great way to review material at the end of a class. They can easily be ended early if time is short. Or, you can extend them if you have too much time by talking together as a class about some of the unusual answers.

Give the students a sheet of paper with some questions and tell them they need to find one of their classmates who will fit each slot. My general rule is that one question equals around two minutes for intermediate to advanced students so 10 questions would equal a 20 minute activity; it's one minute per question for beginners because they will not be as good at asking follow-up questions. The kinds of questions you could put on your paper include things like: "Do you travel sometimes?" or, "Are you a university student?" Then, if their partner answers yes (encourage students to answer in full sentences!), they write down their partner's name and ask them one (beginner) or two (intermediate to advanced) more questions to elicit some extra information. They can only ask each classmate one question. If their partner's answer is no, they should choose another question to ask them.

Prep the activity well before you turn students loose by saying what you're looking for: only speaking English, everybody standing up, talking to everybody in mostly full sentences, writing the answers in English. Get a student to ask you one of the questions first and then ask a student one of the questions so your students have two models of what they need to do. Here is a survey that I would use on the first day of class:

Get to Know Each Other Survey

Name	Do you ____? Are you ____?	Extra Information (W/H ____?)
	from outside this city	
	in third year	
	play sports	
	live alone	
	eat pizza a lot	
	an only child	
	play sports	
	have a part time job	
	have a boyfriend or girlfriend	
	like horror movies	
	in second year	
	take the subway to school	
	think English is the best subject	
	enjoying this class	
	love your school	
	like studying English	

Teaching Tips:

Surveys are an excellent way for students to practice some important speaking sub-skills, especially responding appropriately based on what their partner tells them. For example, if they are surprised they could respond with, "Really?" If in agreement, they could say, "Yeah, me too." If in strong disagreement, they could say something like, "Wow! Why do you think that?" You could even put three categories on the board for "Agree", "Disagree" and "Surprise" and elicit a few ideas from the students about appropriate things they could say in response to a statement.

Another important speaking sub-skill is turn taking. I emphasize to my students that there are times when in-depth and lengthy discourses are necessary (a presentation) but doing a survey activity like this mimics small talk. In small talk, the keys are to listen well, ask some interesting questions and follow-up questions, give short, concise answers and not to ramble. I will sometimes give my students an example of a rambling answer and they usually find it really funny, but I hope that they get the point too!

Procedure:

1. Prepare the survey, based on whatever you are studying.
2. Hand out surveys and write up one or two of the question on the board, making it look the same as the handout. Do two example questions with students, one with you asking a student a question and vice-versa for the second one.
3. Students stand up and talk to one classmate asking them one question (any order is okay). If the answer is "yes," they write in the name and ask a follow-up question. They can write one or two words in the appropriate slot based on the answer their partner gave them.
4. If the answer is no, they must ask another question from the survey until they get a "yes."
5. The pair splits up and each student finds a new partner to talk to.
6. The activity continues until the allotted time is finished.

Tic-Tac-Toe

Skills: Listening/Speaking

Time: 15 minutes

Level: Beginner to Intermediate

Materials: Whiteboard

This is a review game for students to play in small groups. I usually make groups of four and then within the group, there are two opposing teams. Have students make a regular tic-tac-toe board in their notebook or on some scrap paper. Put up a list of review questions in a PowerPoint, or give students a handout. The teams take turns answering the questions and if correct, they get to mark a square on the grid with X or O and the first to get three in a row is the winner. The teacher can act as the referee in case of uncertainty about an answer.

Teaching Tip:

This game isn't fun if your opponent doesn't know how to answer any questions or has never played tic-tac-toe before so in order to prevent this, I put students in teams of two, trying to match a higher level student with a lower level one. Hopefully, at least one of the students will be able to answer questions and has some sort of tic-tac-toe skill. If you know that many students will have a difficult time answering the questions, you can put some answer prompts up on the whiteboard or PowerPoint.

Procedure:

1. Put students in groups of four, two teams of two.
2. Students can make a normal tic-tac-toe board on a piece of paper.
3. Put review questions in a PowerPoint, or give students a handout with them.
4. One person from each team does rock-scissor-paper to determine who will go first.
5. The first team has to answer the first question and if correct, gets to mark the board with either an X or O. The other team answers the next question and gets to mark one spot on the board if correct.
6. The first team to get three Xs or Os in a row is the winner.
7. You can play numerous games and even have the "winners" move up and the "losers" move down like in King's court until you have one final team that is the "King."

Typhoon

Skills: Listening/Speaking

Time: 30 minutes

Level: Beginner to Intermediate

Materials: Whiteboard and questions

This is a fun review game that any age group of students will love that requires a little preparation but no materials. Every single time I play it, my students always want to play again and talk about it for the rest of the semester. Draw a grid on the board, marking one row with numbers and one with letters. 5x5 works well for a 30 minute game. Put in two or three of each of the special letters (T/H/V), secretly on your master paper, but not the board. On the board will just be a blank grid.

T = typhoon: lose all your points

H = hurricane: pick 1 team for minus 5 points

V = vacation: get 5 points for free

E = easy question: 1 point

M = medium question: 3 points

D = difficult question: 5 points

Fill in the rest of your grid with these easy, medium and difficult questions. Then depending on how big your class is, make 4-5 teams. They pick a square, (B-6 for example), then you write the letter in the box and ask them the question or reveal the "special square" that corresponds to it. Have a list of easy/medium/hard questions prepared beforehand. If they get the question correct, give them the points and if not, erase the letter in the box and another team can pick that square if they want and get the same question.

Teaching Tips:

If one team is running away with certain victory, you can adjust it on the fly by switching some squares around but don't be obvious about it. For example, if the team who is in the lead gets a vacation or hurricane, you can easily switch it with an easy question. Then later in the game, hopefully one of the last place teams will get the vacation or hurricane instead (remember a hurricane is where that team can choose another team to lose points, therefore reducing the gap).

If you want to make it more fun, you can be kind of dramatic when writing the letter up in the grid on the board. For example, just do the single line-stroke to start off T, H, E, etc. and students will be anxious to know what it is (because the horizontal strokes of each letter are missing). I also often say things, "Ooooohhhh, bad weather is coming." Or, "Hmmmm . . .

the sky is getting very dark."

Make sure that all the students get a chance to participate by saying that once a student on a certain team has answered a question, they can't answer again until all the other team members have. However, their teammates can help them by giving some hints if necessary so that the lower level students won't feel embarrassed or like they're letting down their teams.

Procedure:

1. Prepare review questions beforehand, as well as a "grid" with the appropriate letters marked on it (T, H, V, E, M, D).
2. Write the corresponding grid on the whiteboard, but be sure not to reveal the letters. It should just be blank at this point.
3. Put the students into 4-5 teams. They can rock-scissor-paper to decide who goes first. The first team chooses a square and then you reveal which letter it contains. If a special square, perform that action and if a question, ask the appropriate level of question. If the answer is correct, they get the points and that square is finished. If incorrect, nothing happens and that square remains in the game.
4. The next team chooses a square, performs the action, and so on it goes with the next team.
5. Keep track of the total points and continue the game until all squares are revealed.

Vocabulary Checkers

Skills: Speaking/Listening

Time: 10-15 minutes

Level: Beginner to Intermediate

Materials: For each pair of students: 1 Checker board marked with vocabulary words, 12 checker pieces in each of two colors

This game is played just like regular checkers, but each square a player might land on has a vocabulary word written on it. The student must give the definition to their partner in order to land a piece on a square. If they do not know a definition, they can buy it from their opponent for one piece. As with regular checkers, the player with the most pieces at the end is the winner.

Procedure:

1. In advance, create, print, and laminate checker boards with a vocabulary word written on each square a student might move a piece to. If you don't have access to a large number of checker pieces, laminate colored circles or squares to use instead.

2. In class, divide students into pairs and give each pair one game board and twelve game pieces in two different colors.

3. If your students are not familiar with checkers, explain and demonstrate the game.

4. Explain that in this version, they must give the definition of the word in a square before they can land on that square. If they do not know a definition, they can buy it from their opponent for one piece.

5. As in regular checkers, the player with the most pieces at the end wins.

Teaching Tips:

If there is a large pool of words, use the spaces initially covered by pieces, since a player might move another piece onto those spaces later. If there are only twelve words, use the spaces not covered by the initial set up. Don't put words on the spaces pieces cannot land on.

I am a frugal person so I have only played this when teaching at schools with large supply closets of games and games paraphernalia. I was able to borrow enough checker pieces and simply made a checker board with the vocabulary on my computer and printed and laminated enough copies. If you don't have access to a large number of free checker pieces, I would suggest laminating paper circles or squares in a variety of colors to use as inexpensive markers. Each pair will need twelve in each of two colors, but if you print different colors for each pair, you will have a store of game markers to use for board games.

Whatever kind of pieces you use, have extras on hand, because you can count on at least one getting lost.

Vocabulary Pictionary

Skills: Speaking/Listening

Time: 10-15 minutes

Level: Beginner to Advanced

Materials: Whiteboard, marker, eraser

Optional Materials: Flash cards

This is a great review game with no prep required. Simply divide students into teams and choose which team will go first. That team will choose a representative to go to the whiteboard and he/she will have to draw pictures (I use a pile of flashcards) that their team guesses. The goal is to get as many points as possible in a specified amount of time (two minutes). Then, the next team does the same thing. You can play as many rounds as you wish.

I use this with classes of up to 20 students and it works well as long as no one gets too rowdy. In those large classes, have students sit at tables, rather than individual desks, so that they can work together easily. If you have a large class seated at desks, you should arrange them into groups of 4-5 desks. If you have a class of ten or fewer, just divide them into two teams.

Procedure:

1. Divide students into equal teams of 4-5. Have each team choose a representative to draw.

2. Demonstrate by drawing a picture representing a familiar term on the whiteboard and elicit guesses from the students.

3. The team that correctly guesses the word will go first. The other team representatives will play rock-scissors-paper to determine their order.

4. Have the drawer from the first team go to the whiteboard and show him/her a flashcard. He/she has to draw it.

5. As he/she draws, his/her team guesses the correct word. The drawer takes another card and the team continues to guess. Continue until the specified time is up.

6. Continue until each team has had at least one chance to play.

Vocabulary Poker Face

Skills: Speaking/Listening

Time: 10 minutes

Level: High Beginner to Advanced

Materials: For each pair/ group of students: 1 deck of cards with a vocabulary word and T (true) or F (false) written on it

    This is a variation of Two Truths and a Lie. Two Truths and a Lie is a simple game where you make three statements about yourself: two are true and one is a lie. Then the other people in the group must ask questions to uncover which one is false. Finally, the other people make a guess about which one is the false statement.

In this version, you should prepare a deck of cards with at least two of each vocabulary word (unless you have a large pool of words.) Each card should also be marked as True or False (T or F.) So, you should have at least one of each vocab word on a True card and also on a False card.

To play, divide students into groups of 3-5 and give each group a deck of cards. Each player should be dealt 3-5 cards, according to the deck size, time you have to play, etc. The remaining cards can be placed aside.

The first player chooses one card and places it face down in the middle, creating a discard pile. At the same time, they make a statement to their group using the vocab word. If they have played a True card, the statement should be true and vice versa. The other players can ask up to four questions total to determine if the statement is true or not.

If another player decides it's a lie, the speaker must turn over the card to display the T or F. If the challenger is correct, the speaker must take the discard pile. If the challenger is incorrect, they must take the discard pile. If no one challenges the speaker, the play continues with the next student. The first person to run out of cards is the winner. You can extend the game by having students use the undealt cards to replenish their hands until the deck has been exhausted.

Procedure:

1. In advance, create a deck of cards consisting of at least two of each vocabulary word (unless you have a large pool of words.) Each card should also be marked as True or False (T or F), so you have at least one T and one F card for each word. If you plan on using the cards more than once, laminate them.

2. Divide students into groups of 3-5 and give each group a deck of cards. Each player should be dealt 3-5 cards, according to the deck size, time you have to play, etc.

3. The first player chooses one card and places it face down in the middle, creating a discard pile.

4. That player makes a statement to their group using the vocab word. If they have played a True card, the statement should be true and vice versa.

5. The other players can ask up to four questions total to determine if the statement is true or not.

6. If another player decides it's a lie, the speaker must turn over the card to display the T or F. If the challenger is correct, the speaker must take the discard pile. If the challenger is incorrect, they must take the discard pile. If no one challenges the speaker, the play continues with the next student.

7. The first person to run out of cards is the winner.

8. You can extend the game by having students use the undealt cards to replenish their hands until the deck has been exhausted.

Reading Review Games and Activities

Concentration

Skills: Reading

Time: 10-15 minutes

Level: Beginner to Intermediate

Materials: Concentration cards

This is a memory game designed to help students remember vocabulary words and definitions. Make up sets of cards with words on half the cards and the matching definition on the other half. A total of 16 cards (8 sets of words and definitions) works well. Make enough cards so that there is one set for each group of four students.

Students mix up the cards and put them face-down on the desk in an organized fashion. The students play rocks-scissors-paper. The first student chooses two cards and places them face up on the desk so that everyone is able to see them. If they make a set, the student keeps the cards (they're removed from the game), gets one point and is able to choose again. If they don't make a set, the student places them face-down in the **same spot** (it's a memory game!) and the game continues with the next student.

Procedure:

1. Make concentration card sets of words and definitions (16 cards per set, one set per four students).

2. Have students mix the cards and place them face down on the desk in an organized manner.

3. The first student chooses two cards and places them face up on the desk. If they make a set, the student keeps the cards and get one point. If they don't make a set, the student places them face down in the same spot and the game continues with the next student who reveals two more cards.

4. The winner is the student with the most points.

Correction Relay

Skill: Reading/Writing

Time: 10+ minutes

Level: High-Beginner to Intermediate

Materials: Worksheet

This is an activity that uses speed and competition to make something old (error correction) new again. Students of all levels should be quite familiar with finding and correcting errors in sentences. By adding a relay aspect, it will (hopefully) make an important but sometimes tedious skill new and more interesting.

To prepare the activity, create a worksheet with 10-15 errors. You can focus your errors on one aspect of vocabulary, such as synonyms and antonyms, or more simply, misuse vocabulary words in sentences. For lower level students, limit the errors to one per sentence. Higher levels can handle multiple errors in one sentence, and you can increase the challenge by having one vocabulary error per sentence and one or more other errors, such as grammar or punctuation mistakes.

The activity itself is straightforward. Students will work in teams of 4-5 to correct the worksheet as quickly as possible. Each student makes one correction and passes the worksheet to the next person who makes the next correction. They continue to pass the worksheet around until it is complete. You can make it easier by allowing students to choose any remaining sentence to correct, or you can require them to work from top to bottom.

Teaching Tips:

To prevent one student from carrying the rest of the team, do not allow other team members to correct another correction. That is, a sentence cannot be corrected by a second student once someone has corrected it. This also prevents more assertive (but not necessarily more able) students from incorrectly correcting others' work.

Also, to keep things moving along you may want to have a time limit for each turn before students must pass the worksheet along.

Procedure:

1. In advance, prepare a worksheet with 10-15 sentences containing vocabulary errors.
2. Divide students into groups of 4-5. If possible, group the desks to facilitate easy passing of the worksheets.
3. Have students take turns making one correction and, passing the worksheet to the next student to make one correction. They continue passing and correcting until the worksheet is complete.
4. When all teams are finished, go over the errors as a class. The team with the most correct sentences wins.

Disappearing Words

Skills: Reading

Time: 10 minutes

Level: Beginner to Intermediate

Materials: Whiteboard

This vocabulary game is an easy way to force students to keep a set of new vocabulary words in their heads, or to review past words. Write down 10-15 words on the whiteboard and give students 1-2 minutes to study them. Then, if you have a big class, ask everyone to close their eyes as you choose one or two words to erase. Students open their eyes and have to tell you what is missing and where it was. If you have a small class, you can choose individual students to close their eyes and then tell you the missing word(s) after you've erased them. You can either write those words in their spots again or add new words to the mix and continue the game.

Procedure:

1. Write down 10-15 vocabulary words on the whiteboard.

2. Have student(s) close their eyes as you erase 1-2 words.

3. Students open their eyes and tell you which words are missing and where they were.

4. You can write those same words back in, or add new words to the mix in those same spots and continue the game.

Irregular Go Fish

Skills: Reading/Writing

Time: 10 minutes+ deck-building

Level: Beginner to Low Intermediate

Materials: Index cards in two colors, list of words; Whiteboard

This game can be used to review irregular past or irregular plurals. There is some deck-building involved, but it won't take your students too long to make them and get a little extra review in the process.

To begin, write the list of words on the Whiteboard, clearly marking which category each word belongs in (past/ present or singular/ plural) and divide the students into pairs. Give each pair one index card per word, so they can write one category on one color index card and the other on the second color. So, if there are 20 words, 10 past and 10 present, each pair will need 10 color A index cards and 10 color B index cards. Have each student pick a color and a category and write each word from that list on their index cards.

To play the game, students will need to look at the card they have and ask for its other form. So, you may want to begin with a review of the words on the board, because some students will probably only read the words from the list they are copying and may not remember the other form when it's time to play.

When the decks are complete, students can stay in pairs or combine pairs into groups of four. In either case, all cards should be combined, shuffled, and dealt out. Everyone should look for pairs consisting of a past/ present or singular/ plural combination. They should lay any pairs down. Then, they should take turns asking for cards they want. When all cards have been paired, the player with the most pairs is the winner.

Teaching Tips:

If students are playing in groups of four, a quicker game is played by one person asking the whole group for a card; a longer game is played by one person asking only one person for a card.

Procedure:

1. In advance, prepare a list of words to review and two colors of index cards.

2. Write the words on the board, categorizing them by form (past and present or singular and plural).

3. Divide students into pairs and give each pair enough index cards to write each word on one. The two categories of words should be written on different color cards.

4. Review the words as a class.

5. When the decks are complete, students can play Go Fish in pairs or fours. They should combine, shuffle, and deal out all cards.

6. Students should first look for pairs in the cards they have been dealt, then take turns asking for the cards they need to complete a pair consisting of one of each form of a word. For example, "go" and "went." (Each pair should have one card of each color.)

7. When all cards have been paired, the student with the most pairs wins.

Odd One Out

Skills: Reading/Speaking or writing

Time: 5 minutes

Level: Beginner to Intermediate

Materials: Groups of words

You can use Odd One Out to review vocabulary from the previous classes. Write up a few sets of vocabulary words on the whiteboard. I use four in one group, with one of them being the odd one out. For example: orange, cucumber, apple, banana. Cucumber is the odd one out because it's not a fruit.

Procedure:

1. Make 4-6 groups of four words, with one of them being unlike the others.

2. Put students in pairs and have them choose the odd word from each group and also write (or say) why they chose it. For example: Cucumber—not a fruit.

Story Timeline

Skills: Reading/Listening/Speaking

Time: 10-15 minutes

Level: Beginner to Advanced

Materials: None

Optional Materials: Sentence strips of important events in a novel

Extensive reading is an excellent way to build your students' vocabulary quickly, but you and your students probably don't want to spend too much class time reading novels. What you can do is assign a novel for homework and in each lesson, go over unfamiliar vocabulary or situations as well as any number of extension activities. This is one such activity and it can be done individually or in small groups.

A timeline, or chronology, of important plot events is a useful way to have the class briefly summarize the story chapter by chapter. A timeline will help them keep track of the story while providing practice determining important events. With lower-level students, you may want to scaffold the activity by providing the sentences for the students to order.

Teaching Tips:

If you are providing sentence strips, you can add extra, unimportant plot events and have the students select only the important ones to order.

Penguin has six levels of graded readers that include simplified versions of popular novels and classics.

Procedure:

1. (Optional) In advance, prepare sentence strips describing important events in the plot.
2. Have the students either order the sentence strips you have provided or determine the events on their own. If you are not using sentence strips, you can have the class complete the activity orally or in writing.

What's the Main Idea?

Skills: Reading

Time: 10-15 minutes

Level: Beginner to Low Intermediate

Materials: Paragraphs divided into sentences

This activity reviews main ideas and details. To prepare, choose one or more paragraphs from the student textbook and rewrite them as sentence strips. Create enough sets for groups of 2-5 students to share.

Begin by reviewing the differences between the main idea and detail sentences and how their roles in a paragraph. Divide students into groups of 2-5 and give each group one set of each paragraph. Have them work together to determine which sentences are main ideas and which are details. When all groups are ready, elicit the correct answer(s) and discuss how they knew which sentences were details and which were main ideas.

You can add a writing element by having students reorder the complete paragraph(s) and writing them. Wrap up by having a student volunteer read each paragraph in the correct order.

Procedure:

1. Choose one or more paragraphs which have a clear main idea and detail sentences and rewrite them as sentence strips.

2. Print and laminate enough for each group of 2-5 students to have one set of each paragraph.

3. Begin by reviewing the differences between the main idea and detail sentences and how their roles in a paragraph.

4. Divide students into groups of 2-5 and give each group one set of each paragraph. Have them work together to determine which sentences are main ideas and which are details.

5. When all groups are ready, elicit the correct answer(s) and discuss how they knew which sentences were details and which were main ideas.

6. You can add a writing element by having students reorder the complete paragraph(s) and writing them.

Where Are They Now?

Skills: Speaking/Writing/Reading

Time: 10-15 minutes

Level: Beginner to Advanced

Materials: None

This is a post-reading extension activity that can be done orally or in writing. When you finish a novel or story, have the student imagine the main character five or ten years in the future. Where are they? What are they doing? How have the events in the story affected his/her life?

Teaching Tip:

If your student has difficulty, help them with brainstorming. Show him/her how to make a mind map with items such as: relationship, job, hobbies, home, pet, etc. Talk with your student about how his or her own life has changed in the past five or ten years.

Procedure:

1. After reading a story or novel, discuss how the character changed over the course of the story and why.

2. Have your student write or discuss what he/she thinks the character's life is like five or ten years in the future.

Word-Definition Match

Skills: Reading

Time: 5-10 minutes

Level: Beginner to Intermediate

Materials: Cards or worksheet/whiteboard/PowerPoint

Card Version: Print one word or definition per card. You will need one set per student, pair or group. This version is good for pair/small group work and adds a speaking component to the task.

Worksheet/Whiteboard/PowerPoint Version: Create a word bank of current or review vocabulary and a list of definitions for students to draw a line (worksheet) or matching letters and numbers for whiteboard or PowerPoint.

Procedure (Card Version):

1. In advance, prepare cards with one word or definition per card. Print and laminate enough for each student, pair or group to have a set.

2. If you're having students work in pairs or small groups, divide the class accordingly and distribute a full set of cards to each. If students will be working alone, give each student a set of cards.

3. Have students match the words to their definitions as quickly as possible.

Procedure (Worksheet/Whiteboard/PowerPoint Version):

1. Have students match the words and definitions, by drawing a line (worksheet) or matching letters and numbers and writing their answers in their notebooks.

2. Have students trade papers to check.

Writing Review Games and Activities

Adjective or Adverb Modifier Posters

Skills: Writing

Time: 10-20 minutes

Level: Beginner to Intermediate

Materials: A3 or butcher paper with a photo or two attached, one per group; markers

Optional Materials: Timer or buzzer

Students tend to have difficulty with correct adjective and adverb usage. This activity provides chance to review. In advance, prepare several images with a fair bit going on in them, such as people at a park engaged in different activities. Attach at least one image to each piece of paper. Each group of 3-5 students will need one piece of paper and at least one marker.

Begin with a review of adjectives and adverbs. Give and elicit examples until you feel the class is ready to complete the activity. Divide the class into groups of 3-4. Give each group one of the prepared pages and a set of markers. Have them write as many phrases describing the image(s) as they can which contain an adjective and/ or an adverb. They should then circle the adjectives and underline the adverbs.

Give a time limit of 5- 10 minutes. If students mostly seem to be done before the time is up, go ahead and wrap up the activity. Time allowing, have each group display their paper and share their work with the class.

Teaching Tips:

To help students remember which is which, write on the board that they should circle adjectives and underline adverbs.

If you are going to have students display their work to the class, you might want to give more correction than usual as you mingle, to avoid embarrassment or shyness.

If you don't want to prepare images for each group, you can simply display one or two large images for the class to use.

Procedure:

1. In advance, prepare several images with a fair bit going on in them, such as people at a park engaged in different activities. Attach at least one image to each piece of A3 or butcher paper. (Each group of 3-5 students will need one piece of paper and at least one marker.)

2. Begin with a review of adjectives and adverbs. Give and elicit examples until you feel the class is ready to complete the activity.

3. Divide the class into groups of 3-4. Give each group one of the prepared pages and a set of markers.

4. Have them write as many phrases describing the image(s) as they can which contain an adjective and/ or an adverb.

5. Have them circle the adjectives and underline the adverbs.

6. Give a time limit of 5- 10 minutes. Time allowing, have each group display their paper and share their work with the class.

Chapter Response

Skills: Speaking/Writing

Time: 10-15 minutes

Level: Beginner to Advanced

Materials: None

Optional Materials: Printed list of questions

Chapter endings make handy stopping points to check your students' comprehension and build a bit of interest to keep up motivation for the next chapter. These questions can be answered orally as part of a book discussion or written in a reader response journal and then discussed in class.

Some questions you can ask include:

What surprised you in this chapter?

What feelings did you have as you read? What made you feel this way?

What words, phrases, or situations in the chapter would like to have explained to you?

Would you recommend this novel to someone else? Why or why not?

How do the events in this story so far relate to your life?

Which character do you most relate to? In what way?

Which character most reminds you of someone in your life? In what way?

What do you hope to learn about (a character) as you continue reading?

What do you think will happen next?

What questions do you have that you hope will be answered in the next chapter?

Procedure:

1. In advance, prepare a printed list of questions about the chapter.

2. Discuss together in class, or have the students write their answers for homework and you can discuss them in the next class.

Got to Hand it to You

Skills: Writing

Time: 5-30 minutes

Level: Beginner to Advanced

Materials: Question sheet and answer sheet

This is a group quiz/ review activity. In advance, you will need to prepare a quiz sheet with the questions and a blank answer sheet. If you will be repeating the activity with several classes, laminate the questions sheets and reuse them. Each group will use one answer sheet, but you can give each student a question sheet or have the group share one or two. If this activity is for credit, be sure to include spaces for all group members on the answer sheet.

The activity is simple enough: each group races to be the first to fill in the answer sheet correctly and hand it to you. If there are errors, they must keep working. When all groups have finished or time is up, review the answers together.

Procedure:

1. In advance, prepare a quiz sheet with the questions and a blank answer sheet. Each group will need one answer sheet and at least one question sheet.

2. Have each group races to be the first to fill in the answer sheet correctly and hand it to you. If there are errors, they must keep working.

3. When all groups have finished or time is up, review the answers together.

Haiku Activity

Skills: Writing

Time: 5-15 minutes

Level: Beginner to Intermediate

Materials: None

Depending on your students' L1, they may have difficulty with English syllables. This is one activity you can do to practice. Since the only real rule of writing a haiku is the syllable pattern (5-7-5), they are a pretty low stress for students, compared to other forms of poetry.

Begin by showing the class several haikus and pointing out the 5-7-5 structure. If they are a bit more advanced, you can increase the challenge by having them write about nature, the traditional theme of haikus

As students work, you can mingle and check their syllable count. If it's off, it will be pretty easy to find the problem word.

Teaching Tips:

I like to use this one as a humorous example:

Haikus are easy,

But sometimes they don't make sense.

Refrigerator

(Credit: Internet and T-shirts everywhere)

Procedure:

1. In advance, prepare a few example haikus to demonstrate the 5-7-5 syllable structure.

2. Have students write their own haiku.

3. Mingle to check their work and discuss errors as needed.

Is that Sentence Correct?

Skills: Listening/Speaking/Reading/Writing

Time: 10-20 minutes

Level: Beginner to Advanced

Materials: Blank paper, vocabulary words

This is a sneaky way to get your students to make grammatically correct sentences using the target vocabulary. Start off by giving your students 5-6 vocabulary words. They should be words that the students are quite familiar with already. The challenge in this activity is not the actual word; it's using it in a sentence. Give the students five minutes to make some sentences using those words (one sentence per word). Do not offer any assistance or correct any errors. You can also make some sentences using the same (or different, but familiar to the student) vocabulary words. Some of them should be correct while some of them should be incorrect.

The first student reads his/her first sentence. Discuss whether it is correct or incorrect and why. Read your first sentence and have a brief discussion about whether it is correct or incorrect. The activity continues until all the sentences are done. If you have a larger class (more than six students), you can put students into groups of 3-4 and have them make sentences together.

Procedure:

1. Give the students a few vocabulary words (and, as the teacher, you can use the same words or different words that the students are familiar with).

2. Instruct the students to write one sentence per word while you do the same with your words. Make some sentences correct and some incorrect.

3. Take turns reading sentences and discussing whether they are correct or incorrect.

Make a Sentence

Skill: Writing

Time: 5 minutes

Level: Beginner to Intermediate

Materials: None, or worksheet/whiteboard/PowerPoint

To practice current or review vocabulary, have students make 1-5 sentences.

No Materials Version: Have students use their books and choose a given number of words to make sentences.

Whiteboard/PowerPoint Version: Give students a list of words to use all or some of.

Worksheet/PowerPoint Version: Fill-in-the-blank or multiple choice with a word bank.

Procedure:

Begin with a brief oral review of the vocabulary words you want them to work with and elicit from the students what the words mean.

No Prep Version: Have students take out their books and notebooks and tell them a number of sentences to make using those words. For example, "Turn to page 53, and choose three vocabulary words. In your notebook, write a new sentence using each word."

Whiteboard/PowerPoint Version: Either give students a word list to choose from, or for lower level classes, several sentences with a word bank. Have the students write the complete sentences in their notebooks.

Proofreading/Editing

Skills: Writing

Time: 5-10 minutes

Level: High-Beginner to Advanced

Materials: Worksheet/whiteboard

To keep proper grammar usage fresh in your students' minds, they should practice frequently. This doesn't need to be a full grammar lesson; a quick warm-up activity can do the trick. You can give your students a variety of errors to correct: word choice, word order, punctuation, capitalization, etc. They should write the sentences or passage correctly.

Teaching Tips:

Begin by asking your student a few review questions about whatever rules he/she is practicing. ("When do you use capital letters?" or "What is a run-on sentence? How can you fix it?")

Procedure:

1. In advance, prepare a worksheet. You could even take a previous workbook activity and reproduce it.

2. The sentences or passage should practice previously studied points of grammar by having errors of that sort: word choice, word order, punctuation, capitalization, etc.

3. Have the students correct the errors.

Review Race

Skill: Writing

Time: 5 minutes

Level: Beginner to Intermediate

Materials: Butcher or A3 paper (one piece per group) or whiteboard and markers (at least one per group)

Some students tend to look at each lesson as a discrete unit, forgetting that they are parts of a whole. This activity gets them using what they have learned. It's a great warm up activity. I've also used it before a test, both to boost their confidence and to give them one last bit of review time.

To play, divide students into groups of 4-5 and give each group at least one marker. If you are not using the whiteboard, also give each group one piece of A3 or butcher paper. Give students a time limit of 2-3 minutes to list all of the vocabulary words they can remember from the previous lesson. With higher-level classes, have students add a synonym, antonym, or brief definition. The group with the most correct words wins.

Procedure:

1. In advance, prepare markers, and optionally, a piece of A3 or butcher paper for each group.

2. Divide students into groups of 4-5.

3. Have students work together to list all of the vocabulary they can remember from the previous lesson within the time limit of 2-3 minutes.

4. For higher-level classes, have students add a synonym, antonym or brief definition of each word.

5. The group with the most correct words wins.

Textbook Part of Speech Race

Skills: Writing/Reading

Time: 5-10 minutes

Level: Beginner to Advanced

Materials: Textbook

Optional Materials: Scanned copy of the correctly completed page to display for students

This is a no-prep part of speech review activity. All you need to do before class is choose a page from the student textbook which is suited to the part of speech you wish to review, i.e.one that has a number of usages of that part of speech. If you are reviewing adverbs or passive, it will probably be a bit trickier than nouns or verbs.

In class, begin by reviewing that part of speech with the class—giving and eliciting examples, etc. Then, have your students open their books to the page you have chosen and have them circle each example of that part of speech on that page. Give them a time limit which will require them to work steadily but thoroughly—not so fast they need to rush, but not so long they have time to get off task. When time is up, elicit the answers from the class. If you have scanned a copy of the correctly completed page, display that for students to self-correct.

Procedure:

1. Choose a page from the student textbook which has a number of examples of the part of speech you are reviewing. Optionally, complete the activity yourself and scan the results to display in class.

2. Begin with a review of the part of speech, giving and eliciting example words, etc.

3. Have students open their books to the page you have chosen and have them circle each

example of that part of speech on that page.

4. Give them a time limit which will require them to work steadily but thoroughly—not so fast they need to rush, but not so long they have time to get off task.

5. When time is up, elicit the answers from the class. If you have scanned a copy of the correctly completed page, display that for students to self-correct.

Vocabulary Roll and Write

Skills: Writing

Time: 5-15 minutes

Level: Beginner to Intermediate

Materials: Dice, vocabulary list

This vocab review activity can be done alone, in pairs, or in small groups of 3-4. It uses the element of chance to make vocab review a bit more exciting. Each individual/ pair/ group will need one die and a vocabulary list.

To do this activity, students will roll the dice as they go down the list. According to the number rolled, they will complete one activity. They should repeat rolling and completing one activity until they get to the end of the list.

The numbers on the dice correspond to the following activities:

1. write the definition

2. write an original sentence

3. write a synonym

4. write an antonym

5. draw a picture

6. write a related word *

* "Write a related word" is pretty general. Students are free to write a synonym, antonym, category (for example, "orange": color or fruit), or something they think of when they hear that word (for example, "desk" study, class, homework, etc.).

When everyone has completed one activity for each word, select a few volunteers to share an answer for each word.

Teaching Tips:

If you don't want 30+ students noisily rolling dice, you can display an online dice roller on your class monitor and everyone can do the same activity for each word.

If you don't want to use all six activities, have two or three numbers represent the same activity.

Procedure:

1. In advance, prepare a list of words to review and enough dice for each student/ pair/ group to have one.
2. If having students work in pairs or small groups, divide them and hand out dice and word lists.
3. Have students roll their die and complete the corresponding activity for the first word on the list. (See above for the list of activities corresponding to the numbers on the die.) Have them repeat until they have completed one activity per word.
4. Select a few volunteers to share an answer for each word.

Worksheet Relay

Skills: Writing/Reading

Time: 10-20 minutes

Level: Beginner to Intermediate

Materials: 2-4 worksheets, one of each per group; timer or buzzer

Worksheets are a necessary evil: students need the controlled practice with new material and textbooks and workbooks don't always provide enough practice in the areas of your students' specific weaknesses. However, their controlled nature makes them pretty boring. Some students will just rush through them with little regard to accuracy, completely wasting their time.

This relay activity tries to address these problems. First, it creates a sense of competition by having students work in teams. Second, most students are willing to work harder to avoid letting their team down than they would just for themselves. Third, the time limit keeps things moving along.

You will need to prepare the worksheets in advance. In class, divide students into groups equalling the number of worksheets. So, each group member will have one worksheet at all times, with no extra students or extra worksheets. Set the time limit for each turn long enough for students to answer one question. For each turn, each student will answer one item on the worksheet in front of them. They will initial their answer. When the buzzer rings, the worksheets should be passed clockwise to the next student. Repeat until all answers have been completed.

When the worksheets have been completed, finish by going over the answers as a class. The team with the most correct answers wins.

Variation:

You can do this activity with one worksheet. Have students sit in rows and complete X number of items (X= the total number of questions divided by number of students in the row.) When the buzzer rings, the worksheet is passed back to the next student. The students can choose which questions to answer, so the students at the beginning have the most choice and the last student has none.

Teaching Tips:

You will want to create the worksheets so that each activity takes about the same amount of time to complete. For example, don't have students creating original sentences on one worksheet and matching on another. Also, each worksheet should have the same number of items.

If you have an odd number in one class, have a lower level student be the extra in one group and have one group member sit out each round.

This is a good activity for an end-of-term review when students are preparing to be tested on a wide variety of material.

Depending on how competitive your students are, you may want to have groups switch papers to check answers.

As always, mingle during the activity. Some students may "help" their group by doing as much of the work themselves as time allows. You should set the time limit so that students have enough time to think then write, but not enough to fill in extra answers.

Procedure:
1. In advance, prepare several worksheets.
2. Divide the class into small groups. Each group will need one of each worksheet. Each group should have the same number of members as there are different worksheets.
3. Each round, each student will have one worksheet to work on. They should complete one answer and initial it.
4. When the buzzer rings, everyone should pass their worksheet clockwise to the next student. Repeat until the worksheets are complete.
5. When the worksheets have been completed, finish by going over the answers as a class. The team with the most correct answers wins.

Before You Go

If you found this book useful, please head on over to Amazon and leave a review. It will help other teachers like you find the book. Also be sure to check out our other books on Amazon at www.amazon.com/author/jackiebolen. There are plenty more ESL activities and games for children as well as adults.

Printed in Great Britain
by Amazon